all that remains

ISBN 978-1-0699577-0-2

for the mother I lost,
from the daughter who remains

Authors Note

My heart compiled all my thoughts
into one spot for all those to see
in hopes to mend others broken hearts.

Disclaimer: tissues may be required.

the seasons

where it still hurts

I am an over thinker,
turning moments over
again and again,
watching anxiety
curl its way into every thought.

I cannot help but wonder,
time and time again,
what if, why, how
each question a small weight
on my chest.

Perhaps one day
this restlessness
will guide me,
but today
it leaves me
shattered,
in pieces.

I became a placeholder
not because he saw a future,
but because it was comfortable.
Avoiding loneliness,
while keeping the door open.
Still, sometimes it felt
he slammed it shut.
And yet, I stayed.

A heart,
shattered once,
rebuild in progress.

I wander often,
but there were signs
quiet, unseen
telling me to stay.

Home was calling,
and that summer,
the sun never seemed to fade.
Six golden months,
time spent with him,
before the leaves began to turn.

Then it was his turn to go.
And now I see
why my gut whispered
to remain
so I could have
that time,
that peace,
that goodbye.

She held on too long after the end,
gripping chaos she called love.
They were never good together
just loud,
and lost.

I tried everything
he kept running the wrong way,
back into the fire
he swore had burned out.

amy burry

No one was safe in their storm,
shelter was not found
some wounds heal,
but that one still echoes.

You speak your desires
like declarations,
while I stand right here
the very thing you want,
blurred by your own blindness.

It's been quiet without him.
The silence of my broken heart
is deafening.

13

Father.
Today, he said,
but it won't last.
It never does.

Almost.

We never dated.
He wasn't a boyfriend.
But he was a secret,
a maybe,
an almost was

He was never mine,
but he was my almost,
my what if,
my only wish,
my never ending thought.

He was the call I kept hoping for,
the feeling I could never name,
the chapter I never got to write.

Tears appear uninvited.
His shadow stays.
My heart aches
deep.

He felt within reach,
real, possible,
not a fantasy I'd lose.
we shared so much
but his heart was
elsewhere.
and mine
unraveled,
broken.

I still cry for my mother,
though she's been gone
most of my life.
Somehow,
she's still here.

amy burry

I find myself
stuck in the same routine,
even long after you're gone.

That empty space
in all the places
you used to be
now lingers quietly,
bringing tears to my eyes.

She longed for it to be over
the pain, unbearable.
Unbeknownst to her,
I watched as she asked quietly,
if she took nothing in,
would it end sooner?

That one moment
is forever etched
in my mind.

He turned to me
when despair set in,
frightened by his thoughts
I helped him cope.

But I felt his pain,
as I always do,
until I found myself
worse off than him,
in need of repair.

I'd had enough.
And when I finally
stood my ground,
it was as if
he had no use for me.

Still valued,
yet somehow
discarded.

The wound is the only route to the gift.

22

She slipped away
as the room emptied
but him.

The love of her life
stood still,
watching the last breath
escape her.

A single tear fell
when we returned,
it was too late.

He showed up for me,
always quick, always near.
then something shifted
I was measured
by his clock,
not my own.
I ache for the old you.

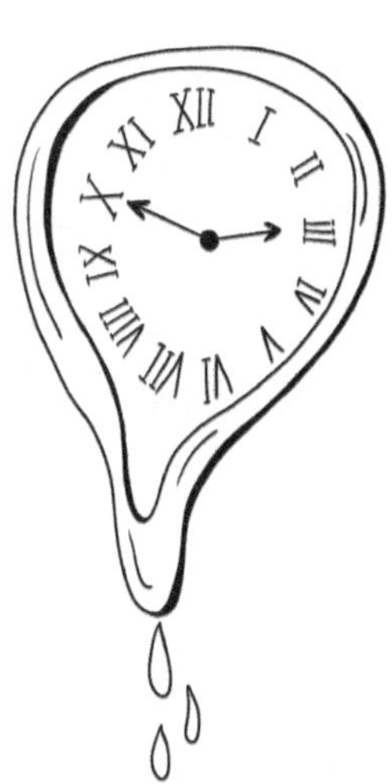

Grief softens with time,
but the love you lost
lingers
a gentle shadow
that never truly leaves.

A heart, once whole,
now fractured,
learning the sharp edges of trust.

She left scars
that whisper in the quiet,
reminding me
that love can wound.

Life is short,
but she spent hers
like a thief in the dark,
leaving behind
a body of ashes
and a heart
unsure of warmth.

And I am left
picking up pieces,
unsure if he'll ever
love again.

She carried the world
on her shoulders
everyone's pain,
their problems.

She felt their emotions,
every heartbeat
that crossed her path

Then there was me
I too felt the weight
of my loved ones pain

At first, it felt like everything hit at once
the sudden quiet,
the space
that felt too big for the feelings you were carrying.
Everything seemed heavier than it should've been.

Then came the loneliness,
the ache of missing a rhythm that used to feel familiar,
an attachment with no place to settle.

Then came the sting of realizing
the energy you once shared
was drifting somewhere else
while you were still trying to make sense of the shift.

But eventually
a breath starts to return,
soft at first, then steadier.

Because deep down,
you know the stability you longed for,
the presence, the follow-through,
the kind of love that shows up
was never going to grow in that space.

And letting go, as painful as it is,
is quietly saving you.

I waited for him to heal,
gave him the space, the guidance, the chance.
But still,
I was hurt,
felt invisible,
like I didn't matter.

It became time to step away,
to breathe, to protect myself.
But he misunderstood
saw my leaving as leaving for good.

Madness and hate spilled from him,
and in that moment,
I realized what I should have done sooner.
Yet my heart clung to hope
that he could be better.

He drew a line,
clear and unyielding
a picture that said
I am never to be heard from again.

One day you'll wake
and feel a quiet disgust,
knowing once
you wanted him
a soft disappointment
in yourself.

I ran to you,
no expectations
just knowing
you needed someone.

Morning light slipped in
as I turned toward you,
resting my head against your chest.
You brushed my hair aside,
kissed my forehead.
For a breath,
I felt love.

But time has a way
of revealing truth—
you were still lost
in yesterday,

and I was left
to gather the pieces
of a heart you couldn't hold

I thought my bout with darkness
was buried in the past
life grew lighter,
brighter in every way.
I reached my dreams,
Every. Single. One.
But then, without warning,
the sky grew heavy,
the rain fell hard,
and the sadness returned.

I stood in the rain with him.
I could have stayed dry.
Instead, I waited,
while it poured,
while he let it—
no umbrella.

She broke you,
and somehow, in the echo of your pain,
she broke me too.
I feel you.   34

Today
should be the day you stop checking
to see if they've seen your story.
Let their memory fade
without feeding the flame.

Stop waiting
for a message that won't come,
stop replaying the *what ifs*
that keep you anchored.

Accept that some souls
were meant to be lessons,
not the destination.

Stop chasing the ones
who keep choosing to lose you,
stop carrying blame
that was never yours to hold.

And then remember—
this release
could have begun yesterday.

I miss the friendship
we once had
before we somehow
lost our way.

I still hope that with
time and space,
we might find our way
back to that place again.

My heart will always
keep a space for you,
even if holding it
hurts sometimes.

We were never
a full story,
just a beginning.

But he reached a place
others never find,
woke a hope
I thought had died.

And losing
what almost was
hurts more
than losing
what ever truly was.

I almost didn't make it,
but no one knew
my breaking point
looked like calm,
my tears
fell inward,
and the pain
that nearly took me
never made a sound.

He is slowly fading away.
The days without him
feel like weeks,
and the distance growing
is hard.

To him… it's nothing.
Meanwhile you sit,
wondering what you did wrong,
forgetting it was him
who made the wrong choice
unaware of what he misplaced.

I'm there for him in the dark,
yet when my lights fade,
he's nowhere
just a ghost.

I built this house
with him in mind —
every choice,
every corner,
was made so he could run,
roam,
and live his best life,
even if his time here was short.

This place was always ours.
Now the house is only mine,
and even stuffed with things,
it feels hollow.

And despite all the work,
all the hours and heart I poured into these walls,
some days
it makes me want to burn it all down
and start again
somewhere untouched
by what used to be.

I lost my friend.
The dynamic I treasured most
the way he opened up,
leaned on me,
made me feel
seen,
special,
needed.

And losing that
is its own kind
of heartbreak
a quiet,
brutal
loss.

The two places I found
comfort
both gone at once.
Now,
everything is silent

He remains,
yet not for me.
I grieve
the man I thought I knew,
the one I thought could be mine.

It wasn't just chatting,
or the easy flirt of words.
He became the pulse of my nights
the late calls,
the quiet comfort,
the way he made space for me in the world.

He wasn't merely a person;
he was a presence
that shaped who I was
when I was with him.

And now,
I grieve not just him,
but the self I carried in his light,
something I thought
was beautiful
and now is gone.

Today was hard.
I needed someone
it was you.
Only you knew my pain,
yet you were nowhere to be found.

I hold myself together,
breathing through the quiet,
and for a moment, I'm okay.

Then something stirs
a thought, a moment, a story I want to share
and you are out of reach.
And suddenly,
I crumble,
all over again.

You carry scars,
from someone who never dropped the blade.
And now you stand here
with nothing left to say.

Compound grief—
my emotional anchor
who held me steady for years
drifted away,
and the other,
here only for a short while,
still became someone
I leaned on.

Both gone,
both losses hitting at once,
leaving my heart hollow,
the weight of it settling
into every quiet space.

Now when the tears fall,
there is no familiar voice,
no steady presence,
no soft place left to land.

Just me,
learning how to hold myself
in the silence
they left behind.

I waited for his voice,
uncertain of its return
each call a small ignition,
each absence
a quiet unraveling.
I felt the truth of it,
but the attachment still deepened
until my heart,
pulled too tightly,
wore thin.

It feels like
he struck the match,
let it flare between us,
and then walked away,
leaving only the warmth
and the ache behind

I'm not angry that you didn't want me.
I understand that kind of truth.
Not every hand is meant to reach for mine.
Not every almost is meant to stay.

What wrecks me
is that you let me believe you did.

You stayed
not fully,
just enough.

Late-night calls that softened my guard.
Pauses heavy with things you wouldn't say.
Breadcrumbs dropped with intention,
each one close enough to keep me walking
through something familiar,
comfortable enough to trust.

You taught me how to turn your *maybe*
into a plan
one that never formed,
one I carried alone.

And I waited like a fool.
In the empty room of your *not yet*,
holding shadows,
convincing myself they were real
because they looked like you in the dark.

You made space in my life
without ever stepping into it.
A presence that felt real
until it thinned—
until you vanished into the fog.

(continued)

You didn't break me loudly.
You didn't say no.
You didn't leave all at once.

You were a slow leak.
A quiet loss of pressure.
Something draining over time
until there was nothing left
hypoxia.

I'm angry at the waiting.
At the pretending.
At the way you stayed within reach
close enough to matter,
far enough to deny it.

Because I mattered
but only as a *maybe*.
Only enough to be kept,
never enough to be chosen.

And that's the damage of it.
Not that you didn't want me,
but that you wanted me just enough
to teach me how deeply
almost can hurt.

turbulence.

53

The wound
was never what broke me.
It was the tending
the slow unearthing
of what had spoiled,
the truth I had to speak aloud,
and the sting I had to endure
so the damage wouldn't spread.
Healing burns in places
breaking only brushed.

falling into pieces

Block Him
They said,
over and over.
But I couldn't.
I held tight to the good,
to the warmth he once gave.

He did care,
once.
When I still mattered.
But as his world shifted,
I slipped out of focus.

I ran for him,
heart on fire,
yet he strolled past,
unaffected

Sometimes,
it felt better
than nothing at all
a hollow comfort,
but comfort
just the same.

If you'd have let me,
I would've loved you endlessly
with laughter spilling
into every corner,
joy echoing off the walls

Our love
would've been loud,
a little obnoxious,
but impossibly sweet.

If only
you'd let it.

Just because
he doesn't have
the same heart as you
doesn't make him heartless,
or cruel
just
indifferent.

Crime is born
from needs left unmet
like a heart abandoned,
it fractures quietly,
and the world feels it too.

Withdrawal
the hold is heavy,
the bond unrelenting.
To break it feels impossible,
yet freedom waits
on the other side.

Just need to be brave
to let someone wonderful
love me,
without fear of being hurt,
without fear
of being safe.

The grief that made me her daughter
was quiet at first
a shadow at the edge of my childhood,
a sigh between the laughter.

I watched her shoulders bend
under the weight of a world
that never slowed down,
and I learned
how to carry the same.

Every heartbreak, every loss,
was stitched into my bones.

I became the echo of her sorrow,
the reflection of her pain,
and in the cracks between her tears,
I found the shape of myself.

The grief that made me her daughter
is mine now, too.

You became the lesson
I finally learned.
I became the love
you didn't choose,
a truth you'll carry
and never replace.

Ambivalent.
half hope, half hurt.
Half love,
half letting go.

Sometimes,
you manifest your life
without even knowing,
and things appear.

When you look back,
you realize you called them into being,
and still,
you manifest more
driven by longing
for that love,
the one true thing
that is still missing.

Eyes searching, prying,
chasing the past
yet the mirror she avoids the most,
reflects her chaos,
her ghost.
Answers elude her
she finds despair.

Take a step forward,
don't glance behind,
the past holds nothing
but what binds.
Looking back will
only harm your mind

Like the sea in calm,
my thoughts grew quiet
and for once,
time stood still.

No matter the miles,
or how our busy days
stretch into weeks,
we still find time
even just a moment
for each other.

Because true friends,
they check in.
No matter what,
no matter when,
they drop everything
to stand by your side.

I've seen it in them,
felt it in their hearts
just not in yours.

Airports are their own world,
a tide of emotions
rushing past me
every time I step inside.

On the plane,
joy and sorrow mingle,
threads of excitement
woven through.

Travel carries me,
and sometimes
leaves my heart
quiet,
numb.

I thought he was perfect,
but I've learned there's no such thing.
There's only two willing hearts
ready to do the work.
Love won't simply fall into place
and stay flawless
perfection doesn't exist.
But one day, it will feel like it,
and then you'll know.

The War
The battle rages, never ending,
each side searching for some mending.
A cold war dressed in quiet pain,
two sides, but no one left to gain.
They pull the others in their hold,
A cycle fought, yet never told

Sometimes the best closure
is silence
it rings the loudest.

75

Never rely on a man.
I listened. I lived it.
Alone, sometimes lonely…
Maybe I took it too far

I love you,
but I'm not in love with you.
Let this be a kindness,
not a wound.

Like cold molasses
climbing uphill
they say
that's the speed
my heart takes
to heal.

You can love
and be loved too.
Don't turn away
let them.

The less he gave,
The more I wanted.
But was it what I needed?
The pull
When really, it was a push.

amy burry

The leaves turned gold,
and so did goodbye
he faded with the season.

Sometimes,
you must say many goodbyes
to shed what no longer serves you,
and step fully
into the best version
of yourself.

Affection is a mirage—
seen, but never held.

All he gave me
crumbs.

Tiny pieces
of something
that was never enough
to feed a heart
like mine.

You will be happy
the moment you allow
yourself to be
until then,
you'll keep chasing peace
through disappointment.

I was searching for clarity
in the hearts of those
who find comfort
in chaos
expecting peace
from the storm itself.

Everything in life
is your fault.

You are
what your life is
no one else
holds the reins.

Stop blaming.
You made choices.

Don't be the victim.
Accept.
Learn.
Move on.

We met, perhaps,
at the wrong time.
Yet I can't leave you in the past,
for I've always believed
we were meant to be
more than strangers,
more than memories
we cling to.

Looking back, it feels obvious
but when you're inside it,
your vision softens to fog.

Someone new appears,
and it's easy to think
they were chosen over you.
Your spirit bends under the weight,
but the truth is simple
the new person
just doesn't know them yet.
They'll learn.
And you'll heal.

I'll be the one that got away,
and when the emptiness settles in,
you'll realize
I was the difference.

I carried your lies
like a lifetime on my back.
Let this be
the last
the final burden
I take from you.

Relationships and friendships
are like the seasons.
some linger into the next,
some fade away.
some people are only meant for one season
the season when you needed them,
or they needed you.

If you hurt someone,
and they still show kindness,
wishing you well,
know this:
you may have lost
the very best for you.

Walking away is easy;
the hard part
is when they don't even try
to chase you

I kinda like it when you call
me on the phone
A gentle, romantic
kind of care
you don't find often.

Laughter and joy,
and the tears we shared…
I'll be thankful
for all of it,
but I'll miss it, too.

I'm not her.
I reminded him
again and again.
He pushed me away
maybe by accident,
maybe trying to protect himself
from someone who
would never have hurt him.

And in the process,
he lost me
someone who wanted to see him *thrive*
even more than I wanted to thrive myself.

But he couldn't see that.
He confused me
with the wounds she left behind.

I'm me.
And one day,
he'll see

I wasn't looking,
but then I found you.
I lost you,
and it hurt
because I loved you
in a way I never knew I could.

A pain so deep,
and that's how I knew.

I saw a future
where it could all work,
and I was willing
to make the sacrifices
to let it grow.

I thought through everything
long before the feelings came.
And when they did,
I tried to ask him,
but I never asked enough.

He moved in circles,
giving me glimmers of hope,
so I held on.

But he wasn't there
to build it with me
not because he didn't care,
but because he didn't care
the way I did.

I'll always hold space for him;
our connection was fierce.
But the thought of that space
becoming vacant
makes me weak.

To know love
is to know loss
they arrive hand in hand

When he held me,
a tear slipped free
one he couldn't see,
afraid he'd mistake it
for weakness,
but it wasn't.
It was joy.
Because in his arms,
he held more
than my past
ever could.

I did all the little things today
meant to lift my heart
flowers,
coffee,
small joys I can usually count on.
But still,
I walked back home
with my eyes full
of unshed tears

Don't underestimate
the void your absence leaves.

It's real.
And it matters.

Crying out your feelings
isn't a setback.
It's your body
releasing what it has held
for far too long.

Each tear
is a small surrender,
a letting go
of the weight that pressed
on your chest,
on your heart.

And slowly
the tension eases,
your breath deepens,
the heaviness lifts,
and you remember
how to feel light again.

No, you're the right one.
And everyone else
is only a catalyst
a mirror held up
to the places
you're not free.

He was a labyrinth.
I drifted, unmoored.

I let the door swing wide.
Ugliness isn't ours, just borrowed.
She wore the hues you forced on her.
The heart remains.

Could a quiet friendship stir
a bond with the enemy,
this may calm our souls.

amy burry

If you think of me,
I hope it's warm
from the days when trust
still lived between us,
before the cold changed you
into someone my love
was never meant to reach again.

Maybe one day
you'll sit with the weight
of everything you kept quiet,
and finally understand
what it cost.

Maybe one day
you'll try to open up to someone new,
and the words will catch in your throat,
because you'll remember
how I always listened
before you ever asked me to.

Maybe one day
you'll see me moving forward
with someone who doesn't hesitate,
and something inside you will shift
not out of jealousy,
but recognition.

Maybe one day
you'll reach for your phone
out of habit,
then stop yourself,
realizing the moment has long passed.

By then,
I won't be wondering
if you think of me,
or if you ever missed what we almost had.
I'll be somewhere new,
no longer waiting for someone
who wasn't ready to stay.

I'll be living the life
I kept putting on hold
while hoping you'd meet me
where I stood.

amy burry

We rush ahead,
lost in the stride,
forgetting to pause
to turn,
to look behind,
to see
if they're even
coming with us.

Breathe.
This isn't your ending,
but the quiet start
of something greater

you were always blooming

Know your worth
it's the foundation
of every boundary,
every dream,
and every love
you choose to keep.

Heartbreak.
It's not just romantic.
It's grief.
The loss of family,
the fading of friendships,
the mourning
of what is no longer ours.

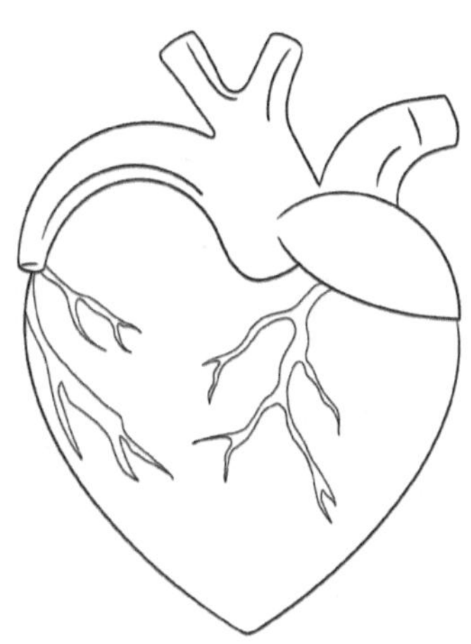

You can only fight
the hatred in others
with love.
they know nothing
beyond themselves,
and your day
is hostage
to theirs.

Run.
It became my escape,
the harder the day,
the faster I fled,
sweeping the weight from my mind.
it gave me clarity
the kind you never could.

New year.
New start.
I won't let what happened to my heart
to repeat.
I won't skip another beat
another year for me,
for no one else.
Then, I'll begin again.

Thank you for revealing
how heartbreak's weight
can explode and reshape itself
into unstoppable strength
that propels me forward.

Watching the light flicker
in someone's eyes
eyes that have lived
too long in the dark
is pure magic,
the quiet kind
that feels like hope.

He compliments me,
makes me feel seen.
The pull between us
is magnetic,
undeniable.

Yet I'm still reaching
for the one
who's trapped in his past.
And now, somehow,
I've become him
standing before something good,
something real,
still craving what I can't have.

But I won't make his mistake.
I'll choose the one
who chooses me.
I'll take this chance
to feel the kind of love
that doesn't hide.

When you move
with good intentions,
karma will find you,
wrap you in her grace.
She, too,
can be kind.

Twenty Twenty-Six
this is our year,
to gently move on,
to leave the ache behind.
A new chapter opens slowly,
welcoming love,
and laughter once more.

It's okay to talk
about grief—
to speak the ache aloud.

Shared stories
of loss and love
lighten the weight we carry.

To heal,
we must share
with those who've felt the same;
it does the soul
only good.

Childless,
but my heart still holds
a universe of love.
Not in absence,
but in strength
I bloom anyway.

Watching contrails fade
is like watching the past dissolve,
a silver thread stretching behind me
as I move forward.

The things I once dreaded most
fall away,
trailing quietly into nothing,
leaving only sky and possibility.

When I arrive,
a complete stranger
calls out *my love* in passing.

It catches me off guard
a small shock of wonder
in the streets I once knew,
in the place I called home.

They showed up. They listened.
No questions asked.
They arrived, steady and fast.
Grief taught me
who my true friends are.

Coffee and chats,
a quiet kind of therapy.

Morning catch-ups
on crisp fall days
exactly what
my soul ordered.

I felt beautiful.
Once you left,
I chose me
for the first time.

Bad things happen,
but they carve a path
that can lead
to a brighter,
happier place.

I gave my heart,
my time,
my everything.
Every word, every action,
every ounce of me.

When it ended,
or I walked away,
there was no regret
only the quiet knowledge
that I had done my best,
and that was enough.

This place is not home,
yet the moment I arrive,
it wraps around me
like I've always belonged.

It's in the golden light
that warms my skin,
the aromas that drift
from every corner,
the pulse of the streets,
the laughter,
the life that hums beneath the sun.

Here, I am both visitor and native
and I am home.

You look nice
Today.

Her first born, gone too soon.
Some days are heavy, dark.
Some days, the sun finds her again.

She lives for him,
she lives for herself,
and still, she thrives.

She is an inspiration
a reminder that no matter how harsh life feels,
no matter the battles fought,
no matter the losses endured,
you can smile again.

I thought it was home,
but it carried a quiet weight,
anxiety woven through every corner,
no matter what I tried.

As soon as I left that rock,
the heaviness dissolved,
only to return
when I stepped back
into a place
that no longer felt like home.

The road you were meant to take
is rarely clear.

There are obstacles along the way,
and people you meet
some that slow your pace,
some that weigh heavy on your heart.

Yet step by step,
through twists and turns,
you move closer
to your destination.

One day he'll return,
but my heart couldn't wait
it was already too late.

She wasn't my mother
but she stood by my side,
a quiet strength
when the world felt loud.

She faced the ones
who stood in my way,
felt my pain
as if it were her own.

She held me close
through storms I couldn't name,
stood in as a mother
when I needed one most.

She stepped forward,
no questions asked,
and filled the space
that once felt impossible
to fill.

He said, *let's be friend*
a shock,
perhaps bold of me,
young, full of life,
with so much to give.
I wasn't buying it.

I tried.
The anger filled my soul.
He was no friend
to compare with the ones
I already had.

Now, I look back
and see the signs—
small, quiet hints I once questioned.
Maybe if he had truly wanted me,
it would never have worked.
And in truth,
he spared me

You are valuable.

You always asked,
wondering why some of us
remained untamed
pretty, smart,
and untouched.

It wasn't that our standards were too high.
It's that we built gardens in our hearts,
and some of you came like storms
wild, devastating,
leaving nothing but broken soil behind.

We fell for men like you
and that's why we don't settle
for anything less than what won't destroy us.

answers appear.
little truths slip out.
every piece exposed.
xenial.

Your value is often unseen
until the moment
you turn away

then suddenly,
they notice
what they took
for granted.

Life tests us,
and it's in overcoming
that we discover who we are.

Part of grieving
is the ache of *what ifs*
the quiet weight
of *maybes*
that linger,
until, gently,
they fade.

With him, I feel calm again.
Even though it's new,
something in me knows
this is joy,
not the old ache of anxiety
left by the man before him.

This feels real.
In every quiet, gentle way:
the strong hugs,
his hand finding mine,
the way he looks at me
like I'm easy to choose.
The small check-ins
on days he knows
my heart might be heavier.

With him, I feel sure of myself again
unworried, unhurried.
And no matter where this story goes,
I already know
he's the kind of man
who is good for me.

Don't run.
Walk.
I remind myself again.
Always diving in,
too fast,
too soon
running
when I should walk.

Grief fades,
but love
love stays.

150

He is the question
I never answered
a shadow that lingers,
an echo I let pass,
forever unresolved.

It happens quietly
a shift you barely feel.
And before you know it,
he's no longer a memory,
just a regret.

amy burry

There were places I traveled
that once held only pain.
Instead of erasing them,
I returned
to rewrite the story.

I made new memories,
brighter ones,
until the places I hated
became ones I loved.

Oceans stretch between us,
a continent apart,
yet we always find the time
to whisper our gossip
of the place we both know too well
the place our hearts remember,
but wish never to return.

We walk different paths now,
live lives that do not align,
yet still we carry
the quiet bond
of why we left,
together,
forever apart.

A man ripe in age,
unfamiliar with his own maturity,
hiding behind humor and deflection
his quiet shields.

He's unaware of his selfishness at times,
still learning how to grow.
And I will continue to support him,
even when it hurts,
reminding him softly.
The pain was never intentional.

I see his limitations,
the edges he's yet to smooth.
Still, I hope one day
he'll rise and unfold,
and that I might be,
even in the smallest way,
a part of him
becoming a better man.

I'm so free
I've forgotten
what direction feels like.

Freedom can be
its own kind of lost.

Selfishly, we are often grateful
for the people in our lives.
We rarely consider that we, too,
are in theirs for a reason.
They might be the ones who hurt us,
but perhaps we were the catalyst
for them to become who they needed to be

It's not a risk,
only a chance
one worth taking.

He made me feel this way.
And I can't help wondering
if he did the same to her
the ex he spoke so ill of.

Maybe she isn't the villain
he painted in his stories.
Maybe she's just wounded,
still caught in his orbit,
chasing the chaos
I once mistook for connection.

Some days,
I ache for her too.
Compassion has replaced blame.

Because in the end,
we were both undone
by the same
emotional immaturity.

I love deep
fully,
fearlessly.
That is not weakness;
it is rare.
And now,
his loss

Parts of me wish
I had never met you,
because the hurt
was so deep.

But then I remember
the good
the joy,
the way I loved and cared
for you, even as a friend.

And that, I realize,
is why it hurt so much.

But I also learned
what I was capable of
through the pain.

Universal accidents
wove us together,
even when the world
felt out of rhythm.

It was quietly guiding us,
in its own imperfect way,
toward the moment
this could finally begin.

It took time
longer than either of us expected
but now,
here we are.
It was serendipity.

There's a soft part of me
that wishes I could explain
why I move slowly,
why some shadows linger
even when the room is bright.

Once, I tried to heal someone
by absorbing their storms,
believing love meant
standing unshielded
in the rain.

But this time is different.
This time, someone new
deserves my truth
not my trauma
my heart, not my heartbreak.

Courage is choosing to show up,
to give your whole heart,
even when you can't see
how the story ends.

If you miss me,
just remember
i'm standing exactly
where you pushed me.

I let it happen,
more times than I should have.
But missing you?
I don't do that anymore

I was born to give.
to scatter flowers
even if my garden grows bare.

Each petal I place
fills my heart more than it empties.
Even when the soil is bare,
joy blooms within me.

Perhaps one day
the giving will return,
a wind carrying seeds
back to my door.

But even if it does not,
my heart will always be full
of the beauty I have sown.

In an old town in Italy,
there's a story whispered
through narrow streets.

Women tuck their hopes
onto small slips of paper
and leave them
for the saint to tend.

I left one there once,
full of doubt,
my lack of faith hidden in the folds.

Time moved the way it does
quiet as breath.

And somewhere along that gentle drift,
you appeared
not as an answer,
but as a familiar feeling.

Some wishes, I've learned,
are slow to unfold.

A heart of gold,
so pure, so kind,
she cares for all
who cross her path.
We share the same small joys
laughter, wonder, light.

She mirrors me
in every way,
but I will teach her gently
the lessons that once broke me,
so her heart may never
know the same fate.

Acknowledgements

This book was inspired by Blitzen, my dog, who helped me begin the journey of moving past not only the grief of losing him, but the loss of others, my mom, and the heartbreaks along the way. He truly set in motion life-changing events that gave me freedom and propelled me forward. A dog can change your life.

Thank you to Sam, for the inspiration and encouragement.

Thank you to my true friends—you know who you are. Without you, I would be lost and never heal.

To my family: you are why I live.

To my readers and all mention above I'm grateful for your support in my new adventure. To those who read closely, thank you for hearing what wasn't said.

If you ever wonder…
(page turn)

—yes, it was you.

About the author

Amy Burry is a Canadian poet who grew up in a small town in Newfoundland and now calls Nova Scotia home. Deeply connected to community, she believes in giving back and finding meaning in shared human experiences.

Her love of aviation and travel has taken her to all seven continents, shaping her perspective and inspiring much of her work. Her poetry is rooted in reflection drawn from journeys taken, hearts broken, and the profound loss of loved ones.

This book marks her first step into self-publishing. What began as private journaling to navigate mental health and grief became a lifeline, proof that writing can be medicine. Through poetry, she shares her healing in the hope that others may find their own.